P9-BIU-097

Comforting Little Hearts

Understanding Blended Families

I Have a New Family Now

Written by Robin Prince Monroe
Illustrated by Nancy Barnet

CPH
SAINT LOUIS

Comforting Little Hearts
Series Titles

Why Don't We Live Together Anymore? (Understanding Divorce)

When Will I Feel Better? (Understanding Chronic Illness)

I Have a New Family Now (Understanding Blended Families)

Balloons for Trevor (Understanding Death)

Copyright © 1998 Robin Prince Monroe

Published by Concordia Publishing House

3558 S. Jefferson Avenue, St. Louis, MO 63118-3968

Manufactured in the United States of America

1 2 3 4 5 6 7 8 9 10   07 06 05 04 03 02 01 00 99 98

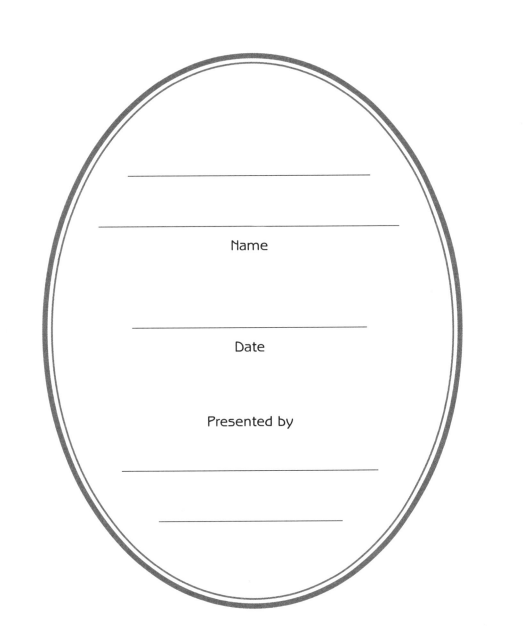

Name

Date

Presented by

In memory of my stepfather,
Gary Granger.
I miss you, Dad.

Families change. New children come into families by birth or adoption. Moms start working or stop working. Children begin school or move away to college.

Families are always changing.

Sometimes families change because of divorce or death. One parent isn't there anymore. At first it's hard, but after a while, you get used to living with just one parent.

My family changed because of _____.

I lived with one parent **most of the time / all of the time**.
(Circle one.)

One thing I liked about living with one parent was _____

_____.

Sometimes families change because of remarriage. Remarriage is when an adult who has been single for a while decides to get married again. The person your parent marries becomes your stepparent.

My mom got married on _____.

My stepfather's name is _____.

I like_____about my stepfather.

My dad got married on _____.

My stepmother's name is _____.

I like_____about my stepmother.

God sets the lonely in families. Psalm 68:6

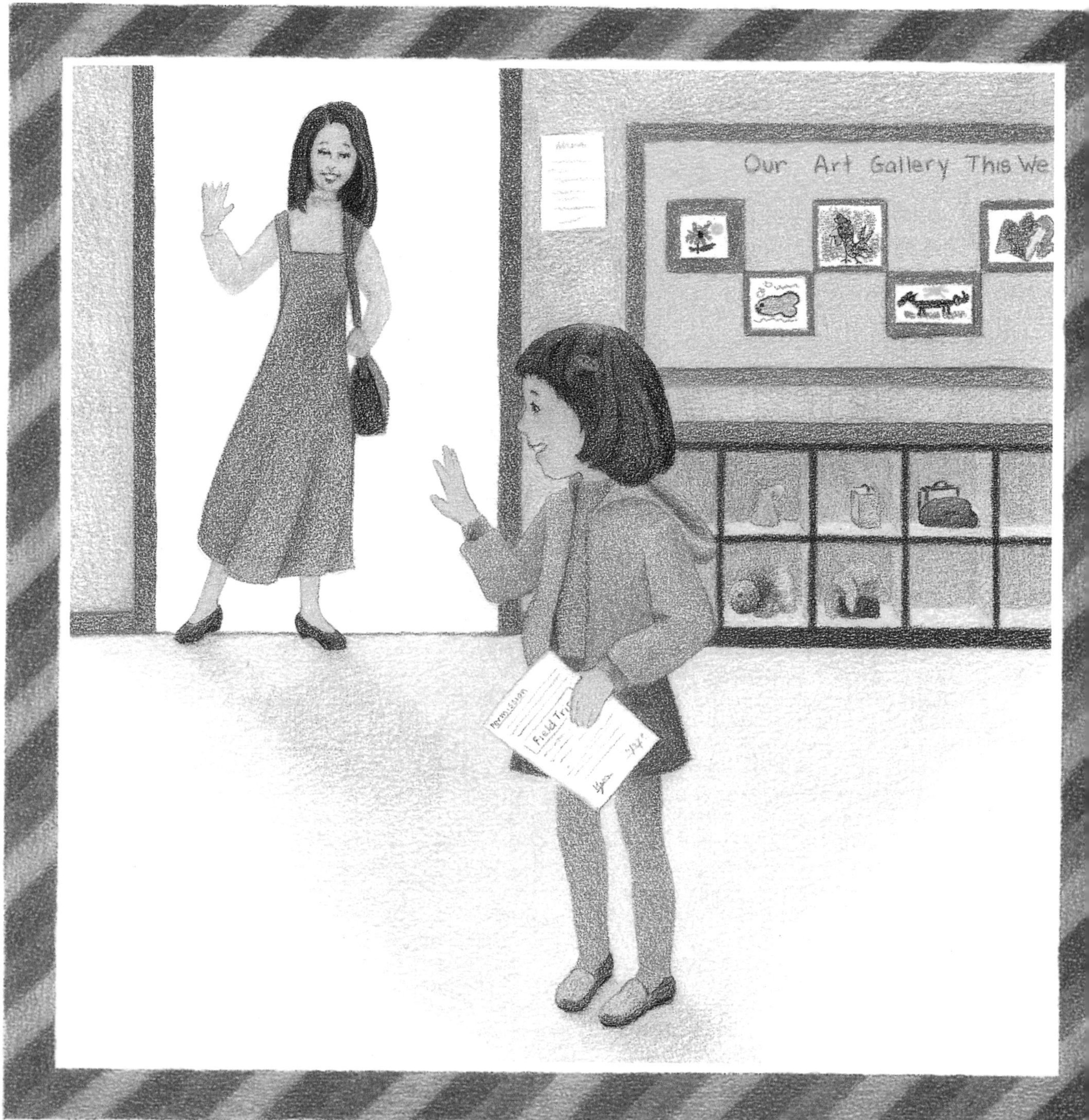
Our Art Gallery This We

If your mom is the one who remarries, her last name might change.

Sometimes that can be confusing. You don't have to explain to everyone why your name is different from your mom's. You can make it your own mystery. (Or tell them to ask your mom.)

After your family becomes a stepfamily, you might not know what to call your new stepparent. It's a good idea to talk about it, then pick out a name that you are both comfortable with.

I call my stepparent_____.

Did you know that Jesus had a stepparent? He did! Jesus' true Father was God, but He lived with His stepfather, Joseph, while He was growing up.

When Joseph and Mary had done everything required by the Law of the Lord, they returned to Galilee to their own town of Nazareth. And the child grew and became strong; He was filled with wisdom, and the grace of God was upon Him. ... "Why were you searching for Me?" [Jesus] asked. "Didn't you know I had to be in My Father's house?" Luke 2:39–40, 49

We have feelings when our families change. Some children feel worried. They imagine how things could go wrong. They may have trouble sleeping.

Some children feel jealous. They might not want to share their parent or their home with someone new.

Some children feel afraid. Their family is different now and that makes it hard to know what to expect.

So do not fear, for I am with you;
do not be dismayed, for I am your God.
I will strengthen you and help you; I will
uphold you with My righteous right hand.
Isaiah 41:10

Some children feel glad. They missed having two adults in their home. They can't wait to start a new family.

Color the picture that shows how you feel.

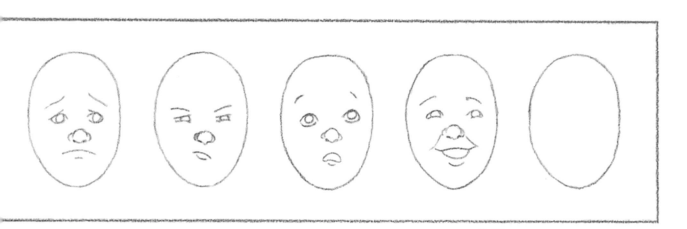

Jesus loves you no matter how you feel. You can talk to Him about your feelings. He cares about you and is always ready to listen.

"For I know the plans I have for you,"
declares the Lord, "plans to prosper you
and not to harm you, plans to give you
hope and a future. Then you will call upon
Me and come and pray to Me, and I will
listen to you."   *Jeremiah 29:11–12*

Sometimes in a stepfamily it takes time to get used to one another. After a while, you may start loving your stepparent. This is great, and it doesn't need to change the way you feel about your own parent.

No matter how you feel about your stepparent, try to be kind and respectful. Then talk about your feelings with your parents or a counselor.

I can talk to_____about my feelings.

Be kind and compassionate to one another, forgiving each other, just as in Christ God forgave you.   Ephesians 4:32

Having a stepparent can mean having
stepbrothers and stepsisters.

My stepbrothers' names are_____

_____

My stepsisters' names are_____

_____

This is what I like about having stepbrothers and stepsisters:

_____

_____

Having so many new people to live with at once can be hard. You might have to share a room or sleep somewhere new. It will help if you can find a little space to make all your own and one or two special toys that you don't have to share. Talk this over with your parents.

My special place is_____.

My special toy is_____.

One of Jesus' stepbrothers was James.
James told many people about Jesus' love.

Isn't this the carpenter's son?
Isn't His mother's name Mary,
and aren't His brothers James,
Joseph, Simon and Judas?
                    Matthew 13:55

I saw none of the other apostles—
only James, the Lord's brother.
                    Galatians 1:19

Draw a picture of your family before remarriage.

Draw a picture of your stepfamily.

Families change. But God **NEVER** changes. He is your loving Father.

God loves you so much that He sent His own Son to die on the cross to pay the price for your sins. You are His special child and He loves you with all His heart.

I the LORD do not change.
Malachi 3:6

How great is the love the Father has lavished on us, that we should be called children of God!
1 John 3:1

How Parents Can Help

by Bitsy Counts,
LISW, LMFT, Family Counselor

Lower your expectations. Stepfamilies are very different from natural families. Expectations for "one big, happy family" can lead to more than one big disappointment.

Go slowly. Allow your stepchild to set the pace for your relationship. Remember that friendship and love develop slowly over time.

Nurture your marriage. Disagreements over children are a major source of conflict in blended families. Focus on your strengths and mutual attraction as a couple. Develop and pursue interests together, apart from the children.

Make allowances for former family structure. Spend time alone with your natural children—time apart from your stepfamily members. Children need to be reassured that they are still cherished by their parent.

Define stepparent roles. You are not and never can be your stepchild's "real" parent. You can't undo hurt your stepchild may have or may be experiencing from a natural parent. Decide with your spouse what your rights and responsibilities will be as a stepparent.

Recognize your child's natural parent. Decide with your spouse how you will deal with your child's other natural parent. It is important to focus together on what is good for the child.

Act, don't react. Plan what kind of stepparent you want to be: accepting, safe to talk to, firm, forgiving, etc. Don't let negative feelings about your stepchild cause you to deviate from the stepparent you have determined to be.

Agree on discipline. Set up rules and consequences that apply equally to all children in the home (custodial and noncustodial). It usually works best for the natural parent to administer the agreed upon consequences to his or her own child.

Accept the prior traditions of each part of the stepfamily. Incorporate differences in taste, style, and holiday observances into your current family regime. A lifestyle that is uniquely your stepfamily's own will emerge over time.

Learn to listen. Allow your children and stepchildren to express feelings of frustration, sadness, confusion, etc. This is an adjustment for them, as it is for you. They may be grieving for their absent parent and their natural family.

Create personal space. It is helpful for each child to have some place in the home to call his or her own. This creates a sense of belonging.

Develop a support system. Isolation is a hallmark of a dysfunctional family. Participate in a church support group or a stepfamily support group. Ask for the help of a pastor or a therapist when needed.

The End